MW01595285

Your Free Gift

I wanted to show my appreciation that you support my work so I've put together a free gift for you.

Download it here: www.bemyguest.pro/art-of-spirits/

Just visit the link above to download it now.

I know you will love this gift.

Thanks!

Table of Contents

What is an Infusion?

Infusions are basically mixtures of liquids, the base of which is often times alcohol. There are various ingredients for infusions such as: herbs, berries, spices and many others. Sugar syrup can be added as a finishing, as well as any additional ingredients. When we consider infusion in its general meaning, we can say that we deal with infusions on a daily basis, because technically, tea is an infusion of plant material in a solvent such as hot water.

In this particular book, we will dwell on alcohol infusions and how we can make nice and unique infusions on our own without special training.

The volume of certain alcohol infusion can reach up to 60%. The process of making alcohol infusion is rather time-consuming and might take anywhere from 3 weeks to 6 months. But the outcome is worth the long waiting period.

Duration of the suspension of the ingredients in the solvent may vary depending on the base for the infusion. During that process, essential oils and other bioactive elements transit into the alcohol.

Spirit is a better solvent for preparing infusions at home, although other hard drinks such as vodka, brandy, bourbon, gin, whiskey, and rum can be used as an alternative. We will discuss that in more detail in the relevant chapter.

In addition to the delectable taste of infusions, we should also mention that they do bear a positive impact on the body. Most alcohol infusions which are used in moderation, are not only harmless to the human system, but on the contrary, they are healthy as well.

History of Alcohol Infusions

Before we begin practicing the preparation of infusions at home, let's take a look at the history of infusions. Infusions have been in use in very ancient times and have a long and interesting history.

It is impossible nowadays to determine the exact date of when the first infusion was prepared, however, scientists do agree that it took place in the area of modern China at the turn of the 3rd and 4th millennia BC. The Chinese have long been known for their medicine, and infusions were often used to treat a variety of ailments.

Europeans of ancient Greece and Rome had already known about infusions. In those places, the history of infusions and their preparation were closely connected to war. Local doctors created a variety of infusions to treat the wounds of soldiers.

Infusions certainly appeared much earlier than balsams, liqueurs, and cordials. Therefore, we can consider them the most ancient among those drinks. Those subsequent drinks first appeared to improve the palatability and or therapeutic effect of infusions. Meanwhile, the introduction of sugar to infusions led to the variation of semi-sweet and sweet infusions.

The history of infusions should be considered primarily as the history of medicine, and secondarily as part of the history of hard drinks. The components that are found in most infusions have long been known for their healing properties and have always been used for the treatment of ailments.

Great strides toward the development of infusions were made possible by the monks. In the middle ages, each monastery had its own recipes for infusions, which were used to treat people who had come to be healed. Furthermore, the monks also tried to improve the taste of infusions and began experimenting with various spices. But because the recipes were kept in secret, attempts at duplicating them failed, which led to the belief that infusions were of divine origin.

Credit should also be given to the efforts of the residents of Piedmont (a territory of modern Italy), which also led to a significant increase in the popularity of infusions. Although the inhabitants of the Alps have long been preparing herbal infusions due to their trade with Eastern Europe, they were now able to make more varieties with tastier flavors.

The popularity of infusions proliferated in the countries with cold climate. In Russia infusions were the result of a lack of variety of wines. And with access to a vast amount of different ingredients suitable for the use of infusions, came the introduction of numerous beverages of that kind.

Gin can be considered the first infusion which became very popular. There was a time when it used to be the drink prepared in every single home in England and Germany. At that time gin absolutely lost its medicinal purpose. On the contrary, the abuse of gin led to the emergence of many social problems, and eventually led to the government's regulation of gin production.

In recent years, the popularity of infusions is increasing. They are continually used both as active therapeutic drinks and as alcoholic beverages. Many bars and restaurants have begun to prepare their own infusions, which often become their hallmark.

Infusions are fairly simple to make, so you can easily make them at home.

Infusions, Liqueurs, Balsams and Brandy: Similarities and Differences

Not everybody nowadays can confidently see and name the difference between infusions, cordials, balsams and liqueurs. At the same time, it is different beverages, each of which has its own properties.

Infusions should be considered the oldest among that type of drinks. As it was mentioned earlier, infusions is an alcohol drink with the volume up to 60 percent which is the result of different herbs, berries, spices and fruits suspended in a solvent - alcohol. Sometimes other ingredients can be added, for instance – syrups.

Cordials have a fundamental difference from infusions. They are produced by fermentation or by adding to the alcohol beforehand prepared juice. In this case, there is a separate allocation of aromatic substances and ethereal oils, while in the process of infusions they transfer directly into an alcohol. That difference is the cause of long suspense for infusions, however, cordials take less time to be prepared.

Cordials are also sweeter and have less volume compared with infusions. Sweet infusions have a volume of 18-25 percent and contain from 150 to 300 grams of sugar. If the drink contains from 300 to 400 grams of sugar for 100 cl that is already called cordial.

If the amount of sugar is more than 400 grams per 100 cl than it is already liqueur. Ingredients are also soaked in alcohol when producing liqueurs. The duration of soaking is less, though than for infusions. Fruits and berry juices or syrups are often included in preparation liqueurs. Liqueurs are quite often distilled and while producing them at home are heated or brought to a boil.

Balsams sometimes are distinguished as one of the varieties of infusions. It should be noted from the two major differences that allow classifying balsams as a separate type of beverage. Firstly, balsams have a thick consistency. Secondly, balsams have more diverse tastes compared to infusions because of a great number of ingredients used for balsams. While for preparing infusions no more than five components are normally used, in the case of balsams the number can reach more than forty.

Healing Properties of Infusions

It is impossible to describe all the healing properties of infusions within one book. Throughout the whole history of humanity, numerous infusion recipes have been created, and most of them have those healing properties. In this book, we will take a short look at them.

Initially, all infusions had a therapeutic effect, because it was for this purpose that they were created. The different effects of infusions on the human body are due to the properties of the components in its composition. Different parts of the same plants can often produce very different effects.

It is important to understand that using infusions as a medication should be followed by clear instructions and small dosages. Although medicinal infusions – tinctures in that instance - had never made people acquire a taste for it, as it is rather bitter, mostly all infusions that are consumed like a hard drink were already adopted for that purpose.

The healing properties of infusions vary. They have beneficial effects on the gastrointestinal tract, heart system, vision, chronic viral diseases, colds, fatigue, and many other problems. It is important to note that certain types of infusions can even provide an excellent relief from hangovers. Herbal infusions have the most useful properties among all infusions.

Base for Infusions

Alcohol infusions can be made with many different liquors as a base: vodka, rum, whiskey, bourbon and others- the instructions for which are quite simple and clear. But according to the original recipes, it is suggested to use spirits in varying volumes instead, which poses a challenge when it comes time to measuring the spirits in the right volume percentage.

For infusions rectified spirits for food use is normally used, which is accompanied by certain properties. It is caused both by the different levels of purity of the products, and the structure of the initial raw materials.

Unfortunately, it is not always possible to define which raw materials in particular that were used for the production of spirits. But if access to such information is available, then it is necessary to give preference to spirits with the highest content of grain.

In order to minimize the cost of the production of spirit, potato starch is often used. It is important to choose the spirits with the contents of starch which doesn't exceed 60 percent, and ideally, is less than 35 percent. Only those alcohols can be used for preparation of infusions at home.

Water acts as another liquid component of infusions. The less the impurity level of water, the better. Spring or deep-well water are the best options, although bottled water or even distilled water is also suitable. And of course, it is better to avoid using mineral water or tap water. The high level of impurity contained in them is bad for the dilution of spirits, and can cause the final product to become muddy.

How to Dilute Spirits

It is very rare for 95 percent volume of spirit to be used in infusions. Most often, recipes suggest the use of less volume of spirit. And that is the difficulty here, because unfortunately, it is not that easy as it may seem to dilute spirits with water in the right proportion.

To have a better understanding of the process of dilution, we need to realize one main rule: the percentage of alcohol in the beverage reflects the volume of pure 100 percent spirit. For instance, 100 centiliters of drink with 50 percent volume contains 50 centiliters of 100 percent pure spirit.

Thus, if we have 100 centiliters of 95 percent spirit, and we looking to get a mixture of 50 percent, then we need to multiply the total by 95 and divide by 50. The result is (in this case, it is equal to 1.9) the amount of the mixture we will get. That means that in order to get a mixture with the volume of 50 percent from 100 centiliters of 95 percent spirit, we need to add water (or rather, add spirit to the water) until the total volume of the mixture becomes equal to 190 centiliters.

In order to make it clear we will use the following equation:

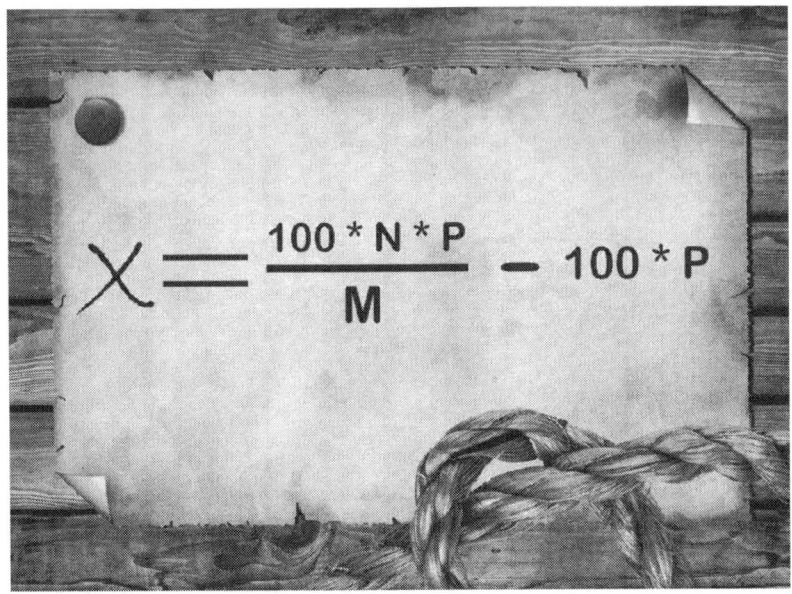

$$X = \frac{100 * N * P}{M} - 100 * P$$

X – amount of water we with which we need to dilute the spirit

N – initial volume of spirit

M – volume/percentage of the mixture

P – coefficient of dividing the initial amount of spirit by 100

If we use this equation for the example above we will get the following:

N = 95

M = 50

P = 1 (since we have 100 centiliters of spirit – 100/100 = 1)

Add data to the equation:

X = (100*95*1)/50 – 100*1 = 90

The result is the addition of 90 centiliters of water to the spirit.

However, it is not enough just to mix those two liquids. We need to follow two very important rules in order to get the right mixture:

1. It is important to dilute water with spirit and not vice versa.
2. Always use cold water, otherwise, the mixture will look muddy.

These rules were first declared by Mendeleev D.I. who has proved that in the combination of 'water-spirit' there are three stable chemical compounds at once. That is why if you pour water into spirit, which is warm, the mixture will turn muddy with an odor of spirit instead of vodka.

How to Suspend Spirits

The last thing that should be mentioned in the chapter devoted to spirits is the suspension of the mixture.

It is not right to start using the mixture immediately after dilution because certain chemical reactions are still going on in there. Therefore, it is necessary to give the resulting mixture some time to suspend.

It is important to fill the container with the spirit as full as possible in order for there to be no free space in it. If the spirit reacts with oxygen, it can cause oxidation and as a result, we will get acetic acid and not the spirit mixture we need.

Basically, the spirit can be used even two days after dilution, but it is better to leave it for a week. The preferred temperature for suspension is 4 degrees above zero or higher. The spirit should be placed in a dark place during that time.

In cases where there is no desire or time to suspend the spirit for a long time, a good solution is to add vodka to the spirit, as opposed to water. In that case, the mixture of the spirit can be used right away.

Main Principles for Preparing Infusions

In spite of the large variety of infusions, there are certain rules that remain constant. Following them will give you the outcome you are expecting and not something else. In this part of the book, we will name some the most important rules.

Time and Temperature

The speed of infusion depends entirely on the temperature that is used to suspend it. The general rule is the higher the temperature, the sooner the infusion will be ready because high temperatures speed up the time of reaction between the spirit and ingredients. It will take 3 weeks for the infusion to be suspended at room temperature, whereas, if the temperature is 50-60 degrees, the infusion will be prepared within 5 days. The method is often used in the process of preparing quick infusions.

Vodka or Spirit?

In most cases vodka can be the wrong choice for preparing infusions. Even if you don't have the spirit in a large amount, it is still better to dilute it with a little vodka. The optimal volume for making spirit infusions is anything greater than 45 percent. That is because spirit is a great solvent, and the greater the spirit content, the better the final infusion results.

Where to Suspend - in a Dark Place or in the Sunlight?

The basic rule for preparing infusions is to keep them in a dark place at room temperature. However, it is not necessary to do so. Infusions can be suspended in sunlight was well. In the presence of sunlight, the taste and flavor changes: the taste will become a little smoked and the color, lighter.

Infusions Made From Berries and Fruits

When making infusions, the useful properties of the solid components get dissolved into liquid form. In order to have the best effect from berries, it is better to freeze them before using in infusions. Freezing will cause the destruction of the structure of the fibers of berries fibers, and as a result, they will produce more juice.

In the case of fruit infusions, frying them prior to infusing, will produce an interesting twist because it will form a caramel coating which will give a more noble taste and color to the infusion.

While Suspending

The lid of the container should not be opened while suspending the infusion because, in the event that the spirit makes contact with oxygen or unwanted bacteria, oxidation will result. There are some instances in which the preparation of infusions involves constant oxygenation, but those are exceptions, and it is always mentioned before production.

Draining and Filtering

Most often the last step in the preparation of infusions will be draining and filtering. For that process, we will need a glass funnel, filter paper, and cotton. The case of the use of cotton, wringing should be avoided, as filtered dregscan fall back into the infusion and the filtering process will have to be repeated.

Storage Requirements

It is best to store the infusion in a very tightly sealed bottles. If possible, it should be kept in a dark room or in a dark glass bottle.

Infusions made from delicate and fragrant herbs or leaves are rather common. These are infusions with a very limited shelf life. This is due to the fact that they quickly lose their flavor and no longer have any value.

Types of Infusions

There are many attempts to classify infusions. Some distinguish infusions based on the quantity of its components, healing properties or the type of the liquid used. Those kinds of classifications are useful for statistical purposes only.

In this book, we will classify infusions in order of the peculiarities of their preparation. Based on that criteria we will determine bitter, spicy and sweet. There is also a group of semi-sweet infusions, but since the process of their preparation is mostly the same as sweet infusions, we will not define semi-sweet infusions as a separate group in this book.

- **Bitter infusions.** These kinds of infusions have a high volume which can often times range from 30 to 60 percent. Bitter infusions are made by suspending the spirit with different kinds of leaves, berries, herbs, seeds, roots and tree crusts.

- **Spicy infusions.** The volume of this kind of infusions is the same as bitter infusions - 30 to 60 percent. The ingredients used are spices- the peculiarities of which determine if there should be extra filtration and distillation.
- **Sweet infusions.** In comparison to the other kinds of infusions, sweet infusions have a relatively low volume of between 18 to 25 percent. They have a high level of sugar which is from 150 to 300 grams per 100 centiliters. Normally they are made by suspending fruits, but other ingredients can be used, and sugar or syrup can be added at any step of preparation.

Basic Recipes for Infusions

In this book, we are going to be giving a lot of interesting and unique recipes of different infusions which will be sufficient for you to use. But if you want to experiment on your own and make something unusual, we have some basic recipes for different kind of infusions in order for you to continue your journey.

Basic Recipe for Bitter Infusions

Before preparing the bitter infusion itself, we need to do some preparation of fruits or berries. Berries are to be washed and dried out and fruits, chopped. Then we pour the ingredients into 2/3 of the container and add spirit or vodka to the brim. In that case, we will be able to avoid the oxidation process.

Use a lid or a thick cloth to cover the container. Depending on the fruits the duration of suspension may vary. But it should still be kept in a dark place. The infusion mixture should be shaken every 3-4 days. After the suspension, the infusion is filtered through a fennel and then poured into a clean bottle. Then store the infusion in a dark and cold place for 2 to 8 weeks, after which the infusion should be ready.

Basic Recipe for Spicy Infusions

Spicy infusions have the same steps in preparation as bitter ones with just the inclusion of an additional step. After the time of suspension has elapsed, the infusion should be filtered and distilled.

Basic Recipe for Sweet Infusions

Sweet recipes have the same steps of preparation as the other types. There are two ways to prepare sweet infusions. One of them is when bitter infusion and very sweet syrup (is mixed with sugar and water in equal proportions) and prepared separately. Then the syrup is added to the infusion in proportion of 25-30 centiliters of syrup and 100 centiliters of infusion. After that the mixture is warmed up to 70 degrees (do not let it boil). When the infusion cools down it should be poured into bottles and kept in a cool and dark place.

The other way to prepare sweet infusion is to mix spirit, fruits or spices and sugar all together and then suspend them. Honey can be used instead of sugar if desired.

How to Prepare Infusions at Home

No matter what kind of infusion you are going to prepare, there are always three different methods of preparing them. Each has its own difficulties and challenges, but the final result is worth all the effort.

The first method to preparing infusion is the most simple. First, prepare all the necessary ingredients: wash, peel, and chop. Then right after pour alcohol and suspend it for the amount of time needed. The last stage is filtration after which the infusion will be ready. In some instances, filtration can be provided twice, but it is not important.

The second method of preparing infusions is by using a concentrated base. In that case, we first prepare the base with some spirit and all the necessary ingredients. After the base has been suspended for the required time, it should be filtered. Then a small amount of concentrate is mixed with the spirit with a volume of 40 percent (usually in proportion of 15 centiliters of concentrate and 85 centiliters of spirit), and fructose is added to it. That process is called blending. After blending, the infusion should be kept for another 3-4 weeks, which allows for the taste to become richer. At this stage, pellets can form. In any case, after blending and suspension, the infusion should be filtered again

The last method of how to prepare infusions is the most complicated but original one. In this procedure, the beverage should be distilled in a cube. To do so, we need to mix all the required ingredients with an aqueous-spirit base of 50 percent. As a result of distillation, we obtain an aromatic spirit. Then the aromatic spirit is diluted with vodka to the desired volume (usually 45-50 percent), and sugar is added. The final step involves suspending again, and filtration if needed.

While it is often enough to prepare infusions according to the first method, infusion prepared on the basis of a concentrated base or aromatic spirit has a more intense taste and characteristic.

Equipment for Preparing Infusions at Home

In order to prepare infusion at home, you will need to get some equipment. For most of the infusions, you will need just a few.

A jar for suspension. To prepare infusions, it is always preferable to use jars made of glass. Although in some occasions the infusions can be suspended in a bottle, it is better to use a jar with a lid that will cover very tightly. In the case that the mixture requires oxygen, the jar should be covered by cloth instead.

A jar for storage. Although it is absolutely acceptable to store the infusion in the same jar used for suspension, it does not look esthetically nice. That is why it will come in handy to have a couple of spare glass bottles with tight lids.

Tools for filtration. The infusion can be filtered in several different ways. Most often, infusions are filtered by using a coffee filter, filter paper, cloth folded in several layers, or a cotton filter.

Tube for pumping. Some infusions precipitate or form an oily layer at the top. To get rid of these undesirable impurities, the infusion is transferred to a new container with a pumping tube. This helps to avoid disturbing an unnecessary layer which can end up in the filtered infusion.

Walnut Membranes Infusions

Walnut membrane is a unique raw material that has been used long ago in order to give a richer taste to beverages which is quite popular today.

One of the most important things to take note of about the walnut membrane is the amount if it that is put into the infusion. There are a lot of recipes in which the amount is different. Careful attention to the dosage is essential, because while some infusion recipes are strictly for medical purposes, others are for beverages.

Although this book is devoted to alcohol infusions, we will still take a look at the topic of medical tincture. You can prepare it by pouring 10cl of spirit into 20-25 chunks of walnut membranes. You should be precautious in the use of it and drink no more than 10 drops a day. This infusion has a lot of useful features, and it helps with iodine deficiency, indigestion, and high blood pressure. It is also good for the prevention of heart diseases, cancer, and impotence. But persons with a history of a high tendency of blood clotting, low blood pressure, ulcers or gastritis should not use this tincture.

And now let's move to more interesting recipes for infusions with walnut membranes. Below we provide three different recipes. Everybody can choose the one he or she likes.

Recipe 1. Basic Recipe for Infusion with Walnut Membranes

This is the simplest recipe, but will still make for a very delicious beverage.

Ingredients:

- 200 cl of 45% spirit;
- 1/3 cup of walnut membranes;
- For sweetness (optional): sugar, honey, sugar syrup, cherry syrup
- For flavor (optional): one-third glass of cherry sprigs, half a plum, and a tablespoon of rosehips.

Directions:

The process of preparing the infusion with this recipe is very simple. Pour the spirit on the walnut membranes and leave it a dark place for a week. Then filter and sweeten with any ingredient you want and allow to suspend for 2-3 days or more (up to a year maximum).

The infusion itself has a nice color and taste, but the flavor is not as strong. That is why one of flavor ingredients mentioned above is preferred for use.

Recipe 2. Spicy Infusion with Walnut Membranes

Ingredients:

- 100 cl of vodka;
- 50 g of walnut membrane;
- 1 clove;
- 2 cinnamon sticks;
- 2 tablespoons of honey (light colored).

Directions:

Put all hard ingredients into a jar and add vodka. Shake the mixture thoroughly. Leave the jar in a dark place for two weeks and mix it periodically. Do not move and touch the jar for the last two –three days in order to allow the sediment to settle in the bottom of the jar. Filter the mixture through a cotton filter and then suspend it for one more week. Because the mixture has cinnamon and honey, it might need one more cycle of filtration before usage.

Although it is always good to suspend infusions as long as possible, with this particular recipe, however, it is better not to overdo it as the infusion can get too many binding substances from the membranes.

Recipe 3. Homemade Bourbon with Walnut Membranes

This recipe suggests the usage of hooch of 50% volume, although 50% diluted spirit will suffice.

Ingredients:

- 300 cl 50% hooch or spirit;
- 1/3 cup of walnut membrane;
- 1 tbsp. black tea;
- 3-4 clove bud;
- 1 tbsp. cumin;
- 1 tsp. oak bark;
- 10 g. vanilla sugar;
- 1 tbsp. sugar;
- Pinch of citric acid.

Directions:

Mix membranes, tea, clove bud, cumin, vanilla sugar and sugar in the jar. Pour alcohol into the jar with the previously mixed ingredients and mix them all thoroughly. There are two stages of suspending this infusion. The first stage: keep the mixture for a week in a dark and warm place and shake it once a day.

Filter the mixture twice after a week of suspension. Use a cloth for the first filtration and coffee or cotton filter for the second filtration. After filtration, it will be nice to sweeten the infusion with sugar syrup.

The second stage of suspension happens when we mix oak bark with the infusion. Soak oak bark in boiled water and then pour the infusion unto it. Cover the jar tightly. The second suspension should last for a month, though it can be extended for up to three years. When you decide to end the second suspension, filter the infusion again and pour in into bottles. Now the infusion is ready.

Varieties of Jan Becher's Recipe

Becherovka is a very popular beverage which is consumed pure or as a cocktail. Although it is impossible to remake the original recipe by Jan Becher at home, it is still possible to make a very similar infusion which will be just as nice.

Ingredients:

- 120 cl of 50-55% spirit;
- 5 g of cinnamon (in sticks);
- 15-20 pcs. of clove;
- 1 g cardamom;
- 2 g of anise;
- 8-10 peppercorns of allspice;
- 1x5 cm of orange peel;
- 150 g of sugar;
- 25-30 cl of water.

Directions:

One of the advantages of this infusion is that it is very easy to prepare. This recipe is for 150 cl of beverage, so it is necessary to have a jar of that volume (it should be a glass jar with a hermetic lid).

First, what we need to do is to suspend the spirit with the spices. Mix the spices and pour alcohol on them. Leave the mixture in a dark, warm place for a week. Shake it periodically. Taste the mixture after 7 days and if it is not spicy or flavored enough, leave it for an additional two days. Once you are satisfied with the taste of the infusion, filter it through several layers of cheesecloth or fine sieve.

Prepare sugar syrup in the proportion of 150 grams of sugar to 25 cl of water. Simmer and stir it until sugar is dissolved.

Let the syrup cool down to room temperature, then pour in the jar and dilute it with the filtered infusion. At this stage the infusion is ready, but it you find it lacks a rich taste and flavor, you can leave it is to suspense for one more week. If the beverage turns out to be too strong in the end, you can mix it with water.

Red Grapes Infusion

Grapes, as well as other fruits, is ideal for infusions. Any kind of grapes can be used for that purpose – sweet, wild or those grown for consumer wholesale. Red grapes are best for sweet infusions.

Ingredients:

- 1 kg of ripe red grapes;
- 100 cl of vodka;
- 300 g of sugar
- A handful of cherries (optional).

Directions:

For this recipe take any kind of ripe, red grapes of your preference. Cherries are optional- for piquancy. If you do decide to use cherries, then prink in so that they would give off more of their properties.

Separate the grapes from the bunch and wash them gently. Try not burst the grapes. Put the grapes into the container that will be used for infusion and sprinkle sugar on top of them. Pour in water and vodka and leave it to suspend. The exact time of suspension depends on the kind grapes used. It can take from 2 to 4 weeks. You will know when the infusion is ready – the grapes will lose their bright color and turn white. When that happens, filter the infusion and pour it in bottles. Suspend the infusion in a cold, dark place for one more week.

Variation*.* For those who want to make a more intense infusion and have the time on hand, there is another variation to this infusion. There will be three stages: at the first stage, pour 70% alcohol to the sugar and grapes, stand for 10 days and set aside. Secondly, fill another jar of the mixture, this time, add in 40% alcohol or vodka, suspend for 3 weeks and set aside. At the last stage pour additional 10-20 % alcohol into a new jar of mixture and suspend for a month. In the end, mix all three liquids together – and the infusion is ready to use.

Clear Infusion of Green Grapes

We also provide the recipe for sweet infusions with green grapes. It will come out clear (almost transparent) but with a very strong taste. For this infusion, we will need sweet, juicy varieties of green grapes.

Ingredients:

- 100 centiliters of vodka;
- 1 kg of green, sweet grapes;

Syrup:

- The peel of two lemons;
- 8 clove buds;
- 2 cinnamon sticks;
- 400 g of sugar;
- 10 g of vanilla sugar;
- 5 centiliters of water;
- A couple pinches of star anise, cumin optional.

Directions:

This infusion is very convenient for preparing at home but will take some effort. First of all, we need to prepare the syrup. Pour sugar and vanilla sugar in a pan and add hot water to it. Boil everything until dissolved but do not let it caramelized. Let syrup cool down. Pour vodka on it and add spices. Chop the cinnamon sticks and break the star anise.

Cover the pan and leave it from 30 minutes to several hours. The longer you suspend the syrup, the stronger the flavor of spices will be. In all regard, it is recommended not to suspend it longer than three hours. That can cause flavor of the spices overwhelm grapes. Filter the syrup afterward.

With the designated jar for suspension in hand, add the grapes, separated from bunches into it, and pour in the syrup to reach the brim. Suspension takes about a month and a half. After suspension, the infusion is ready to be used. Often the infusion is served with the grapes, but it is not recommended. The best way to serve it is to filter the infusion using a cotton filter once or twice and pour in into bottles.

Taste the infusion to see if the volume of vodka and sweetness is enough. Sugar, syrup or water can be added if needed. Suspend the infusion for 2-3 more weeks and then you can enjoy it.

Dill Infusion

Dill infusion is not very popular because of its distinct taste. But it can always be used as a unique substitute for vodka in cocktails, as well as a surprise factor to your friends.

Ingredients:

- 60 cl of 45% spirit or vodka;
- 10 leaves of fresh dill;
- 1 peeled and chopped cucumber;
- 1 tbsp. black pepper corn;
- 1 tbsp. mustard seeds;
- 1 garlic clove small.

Directions:

It does not take very much to prepare dill infusions. Anybody will be able to handle it. Add all the ingredients to a glass made jar and pour in spirit or vodka to the brim. Store the infusion in a dark place at room temperature for a week. Shake it once a day. Then filter it with a fine sieve and pour it into a bottle that closes tightly.

Pure infusion itself is hardly ever nice to drink, but it can be an exceptional addition to cocktails and some varieties of soup. It can be quite interesting to substitute plain vodka in Bloody Mary with dill infusion. It will give the famous cocktail an unusual twist.

Hot Pepper Brandy Infusions

Pepper infusion or pepper-brandy is one of the most unique and unusual infusions. It is not only nice as a beverage, but it also contains healing properties that are good for flu and flu prevention.

There are a lot of recipes for pepper infusions, and yet all of them have two main ingredients – pepper and alcohol. It should be noted that it is very difficult to make pepper infusion with the same taste because of the pepper and how hot it is. It is very important not to overdo the addition of pepper because it can make the infusion too spicy. That is why it is necessary to taste the infusion every day while it is suspending, so as not to miss the time when it is ready.

Recipe 1. Basic Pepper Infusion

Ingredients:

- 100 cl 45% spirit or vodka;
- 3-4 red hot peppers;
- 1cm cinnamon;
- A pinch of propolis;
- 6-7 black pepper corns;
- Lemon zest 1*10 cm;
- 1 tbsp. honey;
- 1 tbsp. paprika.

Directions:

In order for a better extraction, it is necessary to make4-5 longitudinal cuts on the peppers. Carefully crush the black pepper corns. Then pour all the ingredients for the infusion into a jar and fill with alcohol. Mix well, put on the lid and let it suspense for a week in a dark, warm place. Mix the infusion once a day and after a week, then let it sit for two days more. Do not touch it.

Since this recipe contains many components which provide the sediment, the infusion should be filtered for several times before usage.

Recipe 2. Pepper infusion 'Lucifer's tears'

This recipe is especially for those who does not want to go through all filtration process. IT contains only hard ingredients that can be easily removed and honey is substituted to invert syrup.

Ingredients:

- 100 cl of50% spirit;
- 2-3 dried chili pepper;
- 1 tbsp. dry paprika slices (the bigger, the better)
- 1 cinnamon stick;
- Inverted syrup (see last page).

Directions:

This recipe is also quite simple. Before the infusion, the pepper should be cut lengthwise and its seeds, stalk, and membrane should be removed. Since the dried ingredients do not infuse quickly, the time of suspension lies between 10 days to two weeks. You can begin to test the infusion starting from the third and fourth day. Until then the pepper will not extract its hot taste.

After suspension, it is still needed to filter the pepper infusion through several layers of cheesecloth. Add 2-3 teaspoons of inverted syrup and let it suspend for another 2 weeks. Pepper infusion, like most other infusions, is an excellent base for experiments, and a degree of deviation from the recipe may provide a good result as well.

Tips on How to Drink Pepper Infusion

One of the most important things about pepper infusion is how to drink it. It is better to serve and drank at room temperature. Cold pepper infusion loses its taste and flavor, while the warm one has a stronger taste of alcohol than pepper. The first shot of pepper infusion normally burns the throat. After the first shot, the rest goes smoothly and makes for a pleasant drinking. Furthermore, it keeps the body warm in cold climates. Please note that people suffering from the gastrointestinal tract and liver diseases are not recommended to drink pepper infusion.

Hunters Infusion

One of Europe's most popular bitter infusions is the 'Hunters infusion'. The ingredients may vary depending on the country, but it always serves as a warming agent during the cold winter days, as well as an aperitif. The origin of the drink is as the name implies – from hunters and herbalists - people who treat ailments with various natural herbal medicines-who used to gather different herbs and make infusions for their own needs.

There are different methods for preparing Hunters Infusion. We are going to provide a recipe which might require some extra effort, but with an outstanding outcome. For that, we will need to prepare a concentrated base and then dilute it. Some ingredients may be substituted with something similar in the absence of one of the mentioned ones.

Ingredients:

Concentrate Base

- 20 cl of 70% spirit;
- 3 g of dried lemon zest;
- 3 g of dried orange zest;
- 2 g of coffee beans;
- 2 g of galangal root;
- 2 g of angelica roots;
- 1 g of clove;
- 1 g of star anise;
- 0.3 g of black pepper powder;
- 0.2 g of red pepper powder;
- 0.2 g of juniper.

- 12 cl of concentrate base;
- 3 cl of white port;
- 0.5 tsp. of fructose;
- 85 cl of 40% spirit.

Directions:

First, we prepare the concentrated base. Put all the ingredients into a jar. Pour the spirit unto it and let it suspend for 2 weeks in a dark place. Filter it through a cotton filter, or any other filter.

At the second stage of preparation, mix all the liquids together; add the fructose to it and shake it properly. Taste the infusion to see it lacks flavor, and add more of concentrate if needed. If the taste is too intense, add the rest of the ingredients in proportion to it.

When the right proportion is found, suspend the infusion for two weeks or more. It will make the taste richer and nobler.

Starka - Unique Infusion or an Old Vodka

The Starka (Stark) beverage was invented in Eastern Europe during the middle ages. Most likely it came about during the 14-15th century in the territory of Great Duchy of Lithuania, which was very famous for its beverages all over Europe. Back then the infusions would be suspended for ten years, even up to forty years at times. We are going to make Stark much quicker.

Ingredients:

Spirit infusion base

- 100 cl of 70% spirit;
- 50 g of apple tree leaves;
- 20 g of pear tree leaves.

Infusion

- 100 cl of vodka;
- 2.5 cl of infusion base;
- 1 tsp. of fructose;
- Vanilla powder – on the tip of the knife;
- 5 cl of brandy;
- 10 cl of port.

Directions:

First, we need to prepare the infusion base with apple and pear leaves. Pour alcohol on the leaves and leave it for a week. When the base is ready, mix it with the rest of the ingredients and suspend it for five more days in a tightly sealed container.

Apricot Infusion with Wine

Apricot is really good for making different beverages – infusions, cordials, and liqueurs. There is a recipe for apricot infusion with white wine which is quite unique and yet will be good both for the appetite and digestion.

Ingredients:

- 15 cl of vodka;
- 0.5 kg of apricot;
- 450 g of sugar;
- 70 cl of white wine (dry) or semi-sweet.

Directions:

First, mix the sugar and wine in a pan let it heat up until the sugar dissolves. Remove the pits from the apricots, add them to the mixture and continue boiling until they look like a thick mass. Turn off the fire and pour the vodka into the pan. Wait until the mixture cools down.

Pour the liquid from the pan into a bottle and keep it in the fridge for a week. If the infusion looks muddy filter, it before use.

Mint Infusion as an Option for Cooling Down

Mint infusions are not that popular nowadays, and therefore, it is not easy to find a nice and unique recipe for it. But yet, it has a big influence, especially during the hot seasons.

Ingredients:

- 50 cl of vodka;
- 10 g of pepper mint dried;
- 5 g of dill seed;
- 3 g of juniper berries;
- 1.5 of ginger ground;
- 1 g of cinnamon ground;
- 15 g of sugar.

Directions:

It is as easy as pie to prepare this infusion. Simply pour vodka unto all the ingredients, and close them tightly in a jar. Shake it thoroughly and let it suspend for two weeks in a dark place. The Infusion will have a lot of little particles when it is ready, which is why we will need to filter it twice. In the first instance, filter it with a cheesecloth and secondly, with a cotton filter in order to remove the smallest particles.

Strong and Spicy Apple Infusion

Apples have always been one of the best raw materials for beverages. Infusions are also quite lovely when made from apples. The best apples for infusions are the harder, stronger flavored ones. It is not obligatory to take only sweet apples. On the contrary, sour apples give a more pleasant taste to infusions. The opinion that only red apples are good for that purpose is wrong. The most important factors are the kinds of the apples and their ripeness.

Ingredients:

- 50 cl of 60% spirit;
- 50 cl of 45% spirit;
- 1 kg of apples;
- ½ of cinnamon stick;
- 2-3 g of vanilla powder.

Directions:

Wash the apples and slice them. Remove the center part of apples and any seeds. Put the apples in a jar with the capacity of 100 cl and pour spirit of the volume 60% over it. Cover it tightly and suspend it for a week in a dark, cool place. Set aside the first infusion and pour spirit of the volume 45% in a new jar, add cinnamon and vanilla to it. Let it also suspend for a week in a dark, cool place. Mix the second infusion with the first. Pour the infusion into a clean bottle and suspend it for two weeks. That is the last suspension.

It is important to make sure that the apples are submerged thoroughly by the spirit so that they do not emerge at the surface, as not to react with oxygen. If they do, they will begin to ferment. If you did everything right, you would get a nice infusion with a pleasant taste and flavor.

Juniper Infusion for the New Year Party

Juniper infusions are rather popular. That is due mostly to the simplicity of preparing it, although it is not always easy at times to find an exclusive recipe for it.

It is essential to mention the peculiarity of juniper infusions. It should be suspended in the alcohol of the desired volume because to dilute the infusion afterward is impossible. Because of the oily structure of junipers, any attempt to dilute the infusion will cause a change in its color.

Both blue and red berries are ideal for juniper infusions (dry berries are used more often, but fresh ones can be used as well). Make sure that the berries are edible.

Ingredients:

- 200 cl of 50-60% spirit;
- 2 tbsp. of juniper berries;
- 2 big tangerines;
- 2 medium oranges;
- 2-3 whole walnut;
- Sugar – optional.

Directions:

First, squeeze the berries and crush the walnuts. Peel the skin off the fruits and squeeze out the juices. Mix the fruit juices, zest, berries and crushed walnuts together. Pour the spirit into a jar and let the mixture suspend for two to three weeks, then filter it.

Prepare the caramel syrup separately. Take 100g of sugar and melt it in 0.5 tsp. of lemon juice. Add 10 cl of water and let it boil until evenly mixed.

Next, add the syrup to the infusion, but not too much – it will make the infusion too sugary. We only need to make it slightly sweet. Stir it thoroughly and let it suspend for 3-4 days.

Black Currant Infusion

The Recipe for Black Currant Infusion is probably the simplest one in this book. Besides, there are a lot of healthy elements in black currants, and that makes the infusion more consciously settling to prepare.

Ingredients:

- 100 cl of 45% spirit or vodka;
- 1 kg of black currants;
- 100 g of sugar.

Directions:

First, we need to prepare the black currants for the infusion. Wash it and remove all the damaged berries. It is recommended to freeze the berries a little for a better infusion. Fully frozen berries are also acceptable for this infusion. In fact, it will make the preparation for infusion possible at any time of the year.

Mix the sugar with the spirit. Put the currants into a jar and add the alcohol to the mixture. Close it tightly and shake well. Suspend it for one to two weeks in a dark, cold place. Then filter it and pour into bottles. Suspend for one to two weeks more, and the infusion is ready for consumption.

Hot Ginger Infusion

Ginger infusion shares the similarity of a refined scent with pepper. A lot of other ingredients can be combined with ginger to give us an absolutely different beverage altogether.

Ingredients:

- 100 cl o f45% spirit or vodka;
- 200 g of ginger;
- 480 g of sugar;
- 24 cl of water.

Directions:

Peel the ginger and slice it into several strips. Add them into a pan with sugar and water and allow boil it until the ginger becomes soft, and sugar, dissolved. Let it cool down a little before adding the spirit and let it all suspend for a month or more.

After the suspension, strain the liquid carefully through a coffee filter or thick cloth. Pour it into bottles. The rest of the ginger can be used for baking. Ginger infusions have a strong pungency, but it is very tasty and flavorful. A good way of enjoyment is to drink it in combination with lemonade or with ice.

Spicy Cherry Infusion with Vodka

Cherry is both a tasty and healthy fruit. It is often used as an ingredient for homemade infusions. Normally, berries are sour, which is why sugar is a must have a component in the infusion. But seeing as how cherries can also sweet at times, it is helpful to first to prepare the infusion and then add sugar or syrup to it if needed.

There is a saying that cherry pits contain hydrocyanic acid, which can cause serious poisoning, but that conception is incorrect. Cherry pits contain likozid amygdaline that breaks down into hydrocyanic acid when it is in the stomach. But that chemical dissolves in the infusion during the 5-6 months suspension period. In that case, there will be no harm in suspending the infusion with the pits. Besides, that provides a nobler taste.

For an unusual twist, substitute ripe cherries with sun-dried ones. If you would like to use sun-dried cherries, then leave the cherries out in the Sun for 3-4 days, or put them in the oven at 60-80 degrees for 3-5 hours.

Ingredients:

- 100 cl of vodka;
- 2 kg of cherry;
- 10 clove buds;
- 0.5 tsp. of grounded cinnamon;

- 0.5 tsp. of nutmeg.

Directions:

Prepare the cherries beforehand. Wash it, sun-dry if desired, and remove all the stems. Prick every berry with a toothpick and put it in a big jar (300 cl jar). Put everything layer by layer – cherries, sugar and spices and then cherries again. That should take almost 2/3 of the jar. Then add the vodka so that covers the berries completely.

The infusion can take place with either a tightly closed jar, or covered with a thin piece cloth tied around the top. The option that covers it the least will make for a smoother taste. The period of suspension is two months. Keep the jar next to the window with access to sunlight. Keep mixing the infusion every two-three days. Filter the infusion with a sieve or several layers of cheesecloth.

Prunes Infusion

Prunes are dried plums of any kind. Prunes as an ingredient is very popular in cooking, but it is also a great ingredient for infusions. Prune infusion has a very specific taste, but it's definitely worth a try. If you try prune infusion, and you like it, it will become a favorite drink of yours, but if you don't, then you may never like it.

Firstly, it is good to mention a few words about prunes. It is important to taste the prunes before you buy it and also to select the prunes with seeds. Make sure that the prunes are not over-dried. You can tell by the seed. If it is good, the seed can be easily removed from the fruit. Just to be safe, it is better not to buy very dry prunes. Most of the times, the extra dark color of the fruit is a sign that it has undergone some extra processing for a longer shelf life.

Ingredients:

- 45% of spirit or vodka;
- 4-5 prunes with seeds;
- 1 allspice pea;
- 3 black pepper corn;
- 1 anise bud;
- 1-2 g of vanilla powder.

Directions:

Crush the anise bud and peppers in order for them to better release their properties. Pour all the ingredients into a jar with the capacity of 100 cl. Pour the spirit into the jar. Mix everything up properly. Cover the jar tightly and leave it in a dark, cool place for 10 days. Then filter the infusion through several layers of cheesecloth or sieve, and pour it into bottles. Allow the infusion to sit for a couple of days before consumption.

Prune infusion can stay in the fridge or cellar for up to a year to a little over a year. If the taste of the drink seems too sweet, let it suspend for an additional 15 days - fruit infusions often require a longer time to become ready.

Cummin Infusion - Kummel

Cummin infusion - Kummel - has a rather long and varied history. This drink is often mentioned in the works of great writers such as Hemingway, Remarque, and Kuprin. Mass production of this drink was established at the turn of the 16th and 17th centuries in the Netherlands using Boles plants. But it was also prepared at the beginning of the 16th century, and probably has its roots from the Baltic area.

There are different types of Kummel recipes, but the three ingredients remain unchanged - cummin, anise, and fennel seeds. Also, it almost always includes orris and bitter orange. Other ingredients may vary. Here is a classic recipe of the infusion which at one time had a great popularity even with Peter I.

Ingredients:

- 350 cl of 50% spirit or vodka;
- 50 g of cummin;
- 50 g of anise;
- 20 g of dill seeds;
- 20 g of orris;
- 30 g of orange zest.

Directions:

Crush all the ingredients manually or by using a mill. Then put all the spices into a jar and pour the alcohol into it. Suspend the Kummel for two weeks in a warm, dark place. Then filter it carefully with a cotton filter or several layers of cheesecloth. The drink can be filtered again if needed.

Pomegranate Infusion and Pomegranate Liqueur

Pomegranates and its beverages have a lot of amino acids, some of which are indispensable. The use of this fruit has a very positive impact on the health. The recipe below can be made in the form of an infusion or liqueur. If you have chosen to prepare the infusion over the liqueur, do not add sugar to it.

Ingredients:

- 75 cl of vodka;
- 3-6 pomegranates;
- 1 lemon zest;
- 1 cinnamon stick;
- 350 g of white sugar;
- 18 cl of water.

Directions:

First, cut the pomegranates and remove all the seeds. Squeeze out the juice. It can be done easily by using a steel strainer and a spoon. Make sure every seed is removed. We are going to use not only the juice but the seeds as well. Meanwhile, remove zest from the lemon. Do it carefully so as not to peel off the white layer with the skin – it will give the taste of bitterness to the infusion.

The container for the infusion should be washed under hard boiled water. Then put the pomegranate, lemon zest, cinnamon stick and vodka to it. Close the container tightly and let it suspend for two to three weeks in a dark, cool place. Afterward, filter the infusion through several layers of cheesecloth and rinse properly.

If you want to make a liqueur, then pour the liquid back into the jar, add sugar syrup and then let it suspend it for 4-5 more weeks in a cool place. Shake it periodically so that the sugar is dissolved. Drain the drink with the help of a rubber hose in order to get rid of the sediment. After that, you can pour the liqueur into bottles.

The shelf life of pomegranate beverages is about 2-3 months before it loses its flavor.

Garlic Infusion

Garlic infusion is considered to be one of the healthiest. However, it is also perfect for large celebrations and small home events. Its recipe is very easy and will only take minimum effort to prepare.

Ingredients:

- 50 cl of 50% spirit or vodka;
- 2-3 garlic cloves;
- 1 red hot pepper.

Directions:

It is very important to select good garlic with a strong scent and taste. So it is better to get the garlic at a local market or directly from the farmers. Bear in mind that the quality of the garlic has a direct impact on the quality of the infusion.

Remove the center of the garlic and chop it finely. Put it in a jar and add the hot pepper. Pour the vodka into the jar. Suspend the infusion for three days in a warm place. Carefully stir the infusion on a daily basis. Then filter thoroughly and pour into bottles.

The infusion is rather strong, which is why it is normally preferred by men. It is not recommended to store the infusion for a long time, as that can cause it to lose its taste and flavor. Rather, it is advised to consume the garlic infusion within the first five days after preparation.

How to Make Aquavit at Home

Aquavit is a very popular infusion in the Scandinavian countries where it was credited. It has many useful properties. At one point it was even given to pensioners in Denmark, as it was considered beneficial to the health. Although nowadays Aquavit production is manufactured in large amounts, it is still quite possible to prepare it at home, because it is in fact just a plain infusion.

Ingredients:

- 75 cl of 40% spirit or vodka;
- 2 tbsp. of dill seeds;
- 2 tbsp. of cumin seeds;
- 2 clove
- 2 tsp of anise;
- 2 tbsp. of minced cardamom;
- 1 cinnamon stick;
- Dried orange zest;
- Dried lemon zest;
- 1.5 tbsp. of sugar.

Directions:

First of all roast all the spices without oil. Then put all the ingredients in a 100 cl bottle and pour spirit or vodka into it. Suspend the infusion in a dark, cool place for two weeks. Shake it several times a day. If the taste will not be intense enough after the two weeks, then suspend the infusion for several days more. When the infusion is ready, filter it with a coffee filter or several layers of cheesecloth. It is normally advised to consume Aquavit cold and before a meal.

Two Unique Recipes for Orange Infusion

Citrus fruits are great for creating a wide variety of infusions. With the use of Citrus fruits, you get not only a tasty, healthy drink, but also a good addition to cocktails. Oranges are one of the best fruits that excel in alcohol infusions.

Recipe of infusion with orange zest

Ingredients:

- 50 cl of 95% spirit;
- 1 kg of oranges;
- 350 g of sugar;
- 90 cl of water.

Directions:

Before you use any citrus fruit, it is important to wash them thoroughly with a brush and detergent. This allows for eradication of preservatives, which are used for the long-term storage of citrus fruit, which may have a negative impact on the health.

After washing the oranges, peel off the zest. This should be done with a special grater or vegetable knife- it is important not to peel off the pith with the zest, otherwise the infusion will come out bitter.

Put the zest in a jar and fill it with alcohol. Leave to infuse for a week and regularly (2-3 times a day) stir the infusion. Prepare the sugar syrup. To do so add sugar in 50 cl of water, and after it has dissolved add the remaining water. Pour the orange mixture (without the zest) in the sugar syrup and keep in the fridge for 3-4 days.

During the time spent in the fridge an oily film will be formed on the surface of the infusion. We can get rid of it by using a straw to pour the infusion into another bottle. Thus, the film will remain on the sides of the bottle. The orange infusion is recommended to be served cool.

Recipe for a unique form of this infusion.

Ingredients:

- 35 cl of 75% spirit;
- 40 cl of water;
- 1 small orange.

Directions:

This recipe for preparing orange infusion is rather unique. You need to get a small sized orange that can easily fit into the jar for the infusion.

Pour the spirit into the jar. Then using threads, wire and needles, lower the orange unto the spirit, just enough so that the fruit will not touch the surface of the alcohol. Cover the jar and leave to suspend for 3-4 weeks in a cool place. Then remove the orange and dilute the infusion with water. You will notice that the infusion will become blurry. If you want to get a clearer beverage, then let the infusion suspend for about one month.

Tangerine Infusions

Continuing the citrus infusions we would like to introduce two interesting recipes of tangerine infusion. These are nice to drink and very good when you have a flu. In every recipe remember to wash tangerines thoroughly with brush and detergent.

Recipe for Tangerine Vodka

Ingredients:

- 100 cl 95% spirit;
- 50 g tangerine zest;
- 2 tsp. fructose;
- 8.5 cl tangerine fresh.

Directions:

Peel off the zest from tangerines very carefully. Try do not cut the white skin with it. Suspend the zest mixed with the spirit for three weeks (vodka of 45% volume and higher can be used as an option in the absence of spirit). Prepare tangerine juice separately. Squeeze about 8.5 cl of juice and store in the fridge for it to become clear.

After three weeks filter the infusion and dilute it to 45%. Add fructose and tangerine juice. That well cause that the infusion will become muggy. In order to make it clear you can add 7.5 cl of 2.5% milk. Milk will curdle and precipitate, and the infusion will become clear.

Recipe for savory tangerine infusion

Ingredients:

- 100 cl 50% spirit of vodka;
- 10 tangerines zest;
- 3 anise stars;
- 2 cinnamon sticks;
- 2 vanilla sticks;
- 625 g sugar;
- 50 cl water.

Directions:

First again we peel off the zest leaving out the white part of the skin. We grind the peel and put it in a jar with vanilla (cut vanilla into two parts along), star anise and cinnamon. Fill it with alcohol or vodka, and leave to suspend for a week, do not forget to stir constantly.

After the drink is ready prepare sugar syrup. When the syrup cools down pour pre-filtered infusion to it. Keep the resulting mixture in fridge for one more week. Then, once again, filter the infusion and bottle it. This infusion should be kept in the fridge. And its life span is up to six months.

Limon Vodka

To end the part devoted to citrus fruits, we will touch upon lemon vodka. It has a nice taste, natural flavor, and is easy to prepare, compared to other varieties.

Ingredients:

- 100 cl of vodka;
- 2 ripe lemons;
- 5 tbsp. of sugar.

Directions:

Remember to wash the manufacturing wax from off the lemons from. Wash it using hard boiled water, a brush and detergent. Hard boiled water will also help to soften the skin so peeling will be easier.

After washing, remove the lemon peel without the pith - the bitterness of which affects the drink. If desired, you can chop the zest. Squeeze the lemon to a pulp until all juices are drained. Put the zest and lemon juice into a glass container for the infusion, and pour all vodka into it. At this stage, add the sugar, but you can skip it if you desire an unsweetened version.

This infusion can be suspended both in a cold and warm place. The suspension period will differ: 1-2 days in a warm place and 3-4 days in a cool place. If you chose to add sugar, you will need to shake the infusion two or three times a day until the sugar it is completely dissolved.

Then filter the beverage through a coffee filter or several layers of cheesecloth, bottle it and keep it in the fridge. Thought the infusion will be ready for consumption, it is best to let it sit for one more day the fridge before it is consumed.

Distinctive Recipe for Anise Infusion

The Anise infusion has quite a long history. It first appeared in the 16th century, when Asian spices were first introduced to Europe. The infusion has a rather distinctive taste, but you might like it.

Ingredients:

- 50 cl of 45% volume spirit or vodka
- 1 teaspoon aniseed;
- 1 teaspoon cumin;
- 2 anise stars;
- 1 teaspoon of sugar or glucose.

Directions:

It will not take too much to prepare the Anise infusion. To prepare this, pour all the spices into a glass jar and add alcohol to it. Keep it in a dark cool place for two weeks. Then carefully strain the infusion through several layers of cheesecloth or a coffee filter. The infusion can be sweetened if desired with a mixture of sugar and warm water.

Anise infusion is good for the appetite and digestion. However, it is not recommended to consume anise infusion in large amounts. Because of the high level of ether oils, it can have a bad impact on the lever, and cause drunkenness quite quickly.

Traditional Russian Infusion "Yerofeyich"

Russia is one of the countries in which there is a very strong tradition of creating a variety of infusions. One of the most ancient and popular infusions is bitter infusion "Yerofeyich".

There is not an agreement on the correct recipe for "Yerofeyich", and so we can safely say there was have never been one. It appeared in the XVIII century as an herbal infusion. Probably it was given its name after the major Russian wine merchant Vasily Yerofeyich, although there are many other versions of its origin.

According to the traditional recipe the infusion is suspended not by alcohol, but on moonshine, which is mostly distilled several times, sometimes even five, so that the level of its purity would be the fineness. To dilute a moonshine of that quality was considered a waste of a product (after too much effort has been spent for its production), and so people tried to soften the taste of the infusion with herbs. Plant choices varied based on the region in Russia in which "Yerofeyich" was made.

Taking into account that the infusion is not only strong, but also very rich with herbal extracts, it should be consumed in small dosages - usually no more than three shots at a time. "Yerofeyich" Infusion is an excellent aperitif and is perfect with dishes served with meat.

Recipe 1. With Tutsan

Ingredients:

- 50 g of tutsan;

- 50 g of pepper mint;
- 50 g of thyme;
- 50 g of centaury;
- 50 g of melilot.

Ingredients:

- 50 g of centaury;
- 50 g of milfoil;
- 50 g of peppermint;
- 50 g of thyme;
- 80 g of galangal.

Recipe 3. Complex

Ingredients:

- 25 g of lemon balm;
- 25 g of peppermint
- 20 g of tutsan;
- 20 g of oregano;
- 15 g of crushed hawthorn berries;
- 10 g of thyme;
- 10 g of melilot;
- 10 g of marjoram;
- 10 g of white betony;
- 10 g of milfoil;
- 10 g of tarragon;
- 5 g of cardamom;
- 5 g of anise.

Directions:

The recipes presented are in the proportion of 1000 centiliters to 50% alcohol or moonshine. A good solution can also be to make a concentrate, suspending these herbs in 100 centiliters of alcohol, and then gradually pour it into pure alcohol in order to more accurately control the level of the saturation of the infusion. All the infusions are suspended for two weeks in a warm place, then filtered very carefully.

It should also be noted that those ingredients can always be adapted, as its history speaks in favor of experimenting with it. Any missing herb can be substituted with something else available which might produce a nice twist to the taste of "Yerofeyich".

Inverted Sugar Syrup

In most infusion there is always a sweet ingredient. Often times sugar, honey or the usual sugar syrup is used for that purpose. But sometimes honey is replaced by an inverted syrup in order to avoid the need for several filtrations.

Inverted sugar syrup is quite similar to sugar syrup, but has its own characteristics. First of all, it is much sweeter and has a slight tartness to it.

The proportions of the inverted sugar syrup:

- 2 kg of sugar;
- 100 cl of water;
- 0,8% citric acid of the sugar weight (in this case 16 g).

Directions:

Mix the sugar and water in a sauce pan and let it boil it. The foam made from boiling the ingredients is to be removed and citric acid added. The acid reaction with the syrup will again cause the formation of foam which should also be removed.

After that, close the lid over the pan and let it cook on low heat for 25 minutes to one and a half hours. From time to time sample it - we need to get a "thick thread" as seen in the picture.

Conclusion

Thank you again for reading this book! I really do hope you found the best recipes for you.

Made in the USA
Middletown, DE
30 September 2017